D1608997

JUSTIN WILSON'S
CAJUN FABLES

Justin Wilson with Jay Hadley
Illustrated by Errol Troxclair

PELICAN PUBLISHING COMPANY
Gretna 1992

To Lynne
She stood behind us all the way,
We garontee.

First printing, 1982
Second printing, 1986
Third printing, 1992

Library of Congress Cataloging in Publication Data
Wilson, Justin.
   Justin Wilson's Cajun fables.
   Summary: A collection of twenty-four traditional
nursery rhymes and fairy tales rewritten with a
South Louisiana Cajun setting.
   1. Children's literature, American. 2. Cajuns—
Literary collections. 3. Louisiana—Literary
collections. [1. American literature. 2. Cajuns—
Literary collections. 3. Louisiana—Literary col-
lections] I. Hadley, Jay, 1947-   . II. Troxclair,
Errol, 1954-   ill. III. Title. IV. Title:
Cajun fables.
PZ7.W69654Ju 1982 [Fic] 82-18568
ISBN 0-88289-362-9

Manufactured in Hong Kong

Published by Pelican Publishing Company, Inc.
1101 Monroe Street, Gretna, Louisiana 70053

Goldilocks and the Three Crawfish

Once upon a time, a long time ago, there were three crawfish who lived deep, deep in a swamp in the spillway. The three crawfish lived in a house instead of a crawfish hole, for they were prosperous.

There was the great big crawfish, the Papa Crawfish, the medium-sized crawfish, the Mama Crawfish, and the little itsy bitsy Baby Crawfish.

One day the Mama Crawfish cooked a whole panful of stuffed crab. Mama Crawfish said to the great big Papa Crawfish, "While we're waiting for our crab to cool, let's take the itsy bitsy Baby Crawfish and we'll all go for a swim in the spillway."

In the meantime, a little girl with golden curls, who went by the name of Goldilocks, was paddling her pirogue through the swamp. She was lost and was trying to find her way home when she came to a clearing, and there sitting right smack in the middle was the prettiest house she had ever seen. She thought to herself, "I wonder who lives here?" She paddled up to the back porch and knocked on the door. No one answered, so she walked in. There in the kitchen, on a table made of cypress, sat three bowls filled with stuffed crab.

Goldilocks thought to herself, "I know I shouldn't be here but I am so tired and hungry from being lost and the stuffed crab looks oh so good." She sat down at the first bowl of stuffed crab and took a taste. "Oh, this bowl of stuffed crab is too hot!" she said aloud. Then she sat down at the medium-sized bowl of stuffed crab and said, "This bowl of crab is too cold!" Then she went over to the littlest bowl of stuffed crab and said to herself, "At last, this bowl is just right." And she ate it all up.

Just as she was finishing the stuffed crab, she looked up and saw three chairs in the living room. There was a great big chair which she had to struggle to get into. "Oh, this chair is too hard." Then she tried the medium-sized chair and said, "Oh, this chair is too soft. It's like pelican feathers." Then, she tried the third chair, which was an itsy bitsy teenie weenie little chair and she said, "Oh my, this chair is just right." Just then the chair fell all to pieces.

Goldilocks thought to herself, "Cher, I sure am sleepy." She climbed out of what was left of the chair and walked downstairs to the bedroom. There were three beds, a great big one which she climbed into with some trouble. "Oh, this bed is too hard," said Goldilocks. She then tried the medium-sized bed. "This bed is too soft." The third bed was an itsy bitsy bed which she had no trouble getting into. She found it so comfortable that she soon went sound asleep.

In the meantime, the three crawfish came back from their swim in the spillway. As they walked into the kitchen, the Papa Crawfish let out such a roar that he sent ripples in the water outside the crawfish house. He nearly scared the Mama Crawfish and the Baby Crawfish half to death. "Who's been eating *my* stuffed crab?" Sure enough some of his stuffed crab had been eaten. Just then the Mama Crawfish perked up. "Who's been eating my stuffed crab?" But saddest of all was the Baby Crawfish who asked almost in tears, "Who ate my stuffed crab all up?"

The Papa Crawfish started looking around the house and his chair in the living room caught his eye. He let out another roar, "Who's been sitting in *my* chair?" So, too, the Mama Crawfish said, "Who's been sitting in my chair?" But saddest of all was the Baby Crawfish who said, "Someone sat in my chair and broke it all to pieces."

Well, this excited the crawfish to no end. They started searching all over the house. They walked downstairs to the bedroom together looking for whoever it was that was eating their stuffed crab and sitting in their chairs.

Once again, the Papa Crawfish was the one to let out a roar that almost put whitecaps on the water in the spillway outside their house. "Who's been sleeping in *my* bed?" Just as the Papa Crawfish finished, the Mama Crawfish asked the same, "Who's been sleeping in my bed?" But, just then the Baby Crawfish perked up and said,

"Look, there's someone sleeping in my bed!"

Sure enough, Goldilocks woke up with such a start that she dashed out of the bedroom, upstairs to the living room, through the kitchen, and onto the back porch. She tripped over the shrimp net, broke the trout line, and landed right on top of the cricket cage. Finally, she got into her pirogue and paddled off into the spillway, never to be seen again.

Jacques and Jill

Jacques and Jill went down the bayou,
To catch some fish for courtbouillon soup,
Jacques fell in and lost his pole,
And Jill she fell in a crawfish hole.

Little Boy Blue

Little Boy Blue come play your fiddle;
The cow's in the barnyard, the pig's in the puddle.
Where's the little boy that looks after the farm?
Fast asleep with his fiddle under his arm.

Little Jacques Horner

Little Jacques Horner sat in the corner
Eating a crawfish pie.
He put in his pinky and pulled out a slinky,
And said, "What a good boy I am, I garontee."

Blackberry Bush

Here we go round the blackberry bush, the blackberry bush, the blackberry bush,
Here we go round the blackberry bush so early in the morning.
This is the way we pick the berries, pick the berries, pick the berries,
This is the way we pick the berries so early in the morning.
This is the way we wash'um up, wash'um up, wash'um up,
This is the way we wash'um up so early in the morning.
This is the way we make our cobbler, make our cobbler, make our cobbler,
This is the way we make our cobbler so early in the morning.
This is the way we eat it all up, eat it all up, eat it all up,
This is the way we eat it all up so early in the morning.
Yum! Yum! Whoo dat's good!

The Three Little Couchons

Once there was three little pigs who lived with their Mother in a house on the bayou. There was also, too, a great big bad alligator, who lived by himself in a house at the head of the bayou.

One day the Mama Pig came up to the three little pigs and said, "Boys, it's time you went out on your own and built your own houses." So the three little pigs packed their grips and left the house. As they were leaving, the Mama Pig warned them, "There is a great big bad alligator who lives at the head of the bayou. He likes to eat couchon-de-lait (dat mean milk-fed pig), so be careful and take care of yourselves." The little pigs told their Mama good-bye and promised to look out for the big bad alligator.

After walking a while, the pigs came to a fork in the bayou. The first pig said, "I'm going down this fork to build my house." The second pig said, "I'm going down the other fork to build my house." The third pig said, "I'll stay right here and build my house." Each pig then started to build his house.

The first pig built his house of rice straw. He was finished in a jiffy and said, "Now I

have time to sing and fais-do-do (run, play, and dance)." Little did the first pig know that there was someone watching him from beneath the waters of the bayou, and that someone sure enjoyed couchon-de-lait.

In the meantime, the second pig was busy at work on his house. He had found some sugarcane and put it up in a jiffy. He looked at the house and said, "It's not the best house in the world, but I like to have time to sing and fais-do-do." Little did the second pig know that someone was watching him too! And that someone sure did enjoy couchon-de-lait (dat mean milk-fed pig).

The third pig was very busy building his house. He was a hard-working pig and was building his house of solid cypress. He took his time and made sure that the house he was building was strong and secure. After a long time and a lot of work, he finally finished his house of cypress. Then he said, "Now I have time to sing and fais-do-do." The third pig didn't know that he, too, was being watched from beneath the bayou. That someone sure did enjoy couchon-de-lait.

The next day, the first little pig was cleaning house and he looked out his window. He had a visitor—the big bad alligator! The alligator knocked and said to the first pig, "Little pig, let me in, let me in." The little pig said, "No, I won't let you in by the hair of my chinny-chin-chin." Then the alligator said, "I'll huff and I'll puff and I'll blow your house down." And sure enough he huffed and he puffed and he blew that house of rice straw right down! Lucky for the little pig he got out of the house and ran down the bayou to his brother's house. "Help, help, the big bad alligator is coming!"

The second pig let his brother in quickly and locked the door. Well, the big bad alli-gator disguised himself in lamb's skin. He went up to the second pig's door and knocked. "Little pigs, let me in, let me in, for I am a poor lost little lamb." But the second pig recognized the gator's snout sticking out of the lamb's skin and he said, "Not by the hair of my chinny-chin-chin." The gator said, "I'll huff and I'll puff and I'll blow your house down." Sure enough, he huffed and he puffed and he blew that house made of sugarcane right down!

The two pigs raced out of the house and down the bayou to their brother's house made of solid cypress. "Help us, brother, the big bad alligator is coming," they said as their brother let them in and locked the door behind them.

Just then, there was a knock on the door. The big bad alligator said, "Let me in little pigs, or I'll blow your house down." The third little pig's brothers were shaking and trembling. "Don't be afraid brothers, for I have taken the time to build a good strong house." The third pig called out to the gator, "Go ahead and blow, we're not afraid." Well, sure enough the gator huffed and puffed and huffed and puffed till he was blue in the face. He couldn't blow that house of cypress down! Poo-yah, was that gator mad! Then the alligator had an idea, "I'll climb down the chimney and have couchon-de-lait after all."

In the meantime, the three little pigs heard the alligator walking on the roof. "Hurry up," said the third little pig, as they ran to the fireplace and built a hot fire. They put a big pot over the fire and waited. Sure enough, the alligator crawled down the chimney and fell right into the big pot of boiling water.

That was the last time the three little pigs saw the big bad alligator. From then on, they were able to sing and fais-do-do as much as they wanted.

Jacques Castille

Jacques Castille
Him, he could eat no veal,
His wife her, she could eat no beef,
And so, between them together, both
A whole cow they could not eat!

Three Blind Possums

Three blind possums, three blind possums,
See how they run! See how they run!
They all ran after the shrimper's wife,
Who cut off their tails with an oyster knife,
Did you ever see such a thing in you life,
As three blind possums.

There Was an Old Man

There was an old man who lived in a boot;
He got so many dogs he didn't really give a hoot.
He gave them gristle and fat and bones to eat;
But him, he kept for himself all the meat.

To Market

To market, to market to buy an etouffe;
Home again,
For shopping is through for another day.

A Crawfish Pie

Crawfish, Crawfish, Crawfish Pie!
Brought yourself ladies, brought yourself and buy.
Else your husbands they gonna cry.

Cajun ABC's

A is for the alligator who lives in the bayou;
B is for the bayou that the alligator live in, also too;
C is for the couchon-de-lait, that's milk-fed pig, that we like to eat;
D is for the ducks that swim on the marsh and fly so fleet;
E is for the egret that flies away;
F is for the fais-do-do, dat a dance, all night and all day;
G is for the grits we eat in the morning;
H is for the hound dog that sleep on the front yard;
I is for the inlet where shrimp boats rest;
J is for Poppa Justin who loves all you children best;
K is for all kids listening today;
L is for landing where we dock our boats;
M is for Mama who loves us most;
N is for Nanny who loves us too;
O is for oysters that we like to eat;
P is for possums who don't like to sleep;
Q is for queens, all so pretty, who reign at dem fair and festivals;
R is for roux that goes in our stews;
S is for sassafras that makes file for our gumbo;
T is for tarpon that swim in the Gulf of Mexico;
U is for umbrella that we use when it rains;
V is for vegetables that we grow in our garden;
W is for the water what we love to swim in;
X is for the xylophone dat the jazz man play;
Y is for you, a very good friend to me;
Z is for the zoo, where dem animal all dance for you.

This Little Pig Went to the French Market

This little pig went to the French Market;
This little pig stayed at his house;
This little pig had jambalaya;
This little pig got nothing at all any,
This little pig said "Wee-wee" all the way to his Mama with a penny.

Pat-A-Cake

Pat-a-cake, pat-a-cake, Crawfish Man;
Bake me a pie, Cher, as fast as you can.
Pat it and roll it and mark it with a "C";
Put it in the oven for Cher, de Babe and me.

Jacques Be Nimble

Jacques by nimble;
Jacques be quick;
Jacques he don't want to jump over that
    candlestick, no!

Beignet Man

Once upon a time, there was a great big Mama and a little old Papa who lived in a house on False River.

One day the Mama decided to cook some doughnuts for Papa. When she finished making the doughnuts, she had a whole lot of scraps of dough left over from the doughnuts. She thought to herself, "I'll make a big beignet." As she rolled the dough out, she suddenly had an idea. "I'll make a beignet man." She then put the beignet man into the grease to cook and turned her back to clean the mess that she had made. When the Mama turned back around, out of the fryer jumped the Beignet Man and headed out of the door. Well, the Mama ran after him, but try as she may, she could not catch him.

He turned back and said to her:

> "Hurry, hurry as much as you can,
> You won't catch me,
> 'cause I'm the Beignet Man, I am!"

Then the Beignet Man ran past the Papa, who was plowing his fields.

> "Hurry, hurry as much as you can,
> You won't catch me,
> 'cause I'm the Beignet Man, I am!"
> I've hurried away from Mama and
> I can hurry away from you, too."

The Papa ran after the Beignet Man, but he could not catch him.

The Beignet Man then came up to a sugarcane field. There were men cutting the sugarcane and the Beignet Man said to them as he went by:

> "I've hurried away from Mama and from Papa
> And I can hurry away from you too,
> 'cause I'm the Beignet Man, I am!"

The sugarcane cutters ran after him, but they could not catch him either!

The Beignet Man ran and ran until he came upon Peter Pelican, who was shading himself under a tree.

> "Hurry, hurry as much as you can,
> I am the Beignet Man, I am!
> I've hurried away from the Mama,
> Papa, the sugarcane cutters
> And I can hurry away from you, too!"

Peter Pelican ran as fast as he could, but he couldn't catch the Beignet Man!

The Beignet Man just kept a hurrying 'til he came upon two raccoons cleaning crawfish in a clearing.

> "I've hurried from the Mama,
> Papa, the sugarcane cutters,
> And Peter Pelican,
> And I can hurry away from you too,
> I can!"

The raccoons dropped their crawfish and hurried after the Beignet Man, but they could not catch him.

The Beignet Man kept hurrying until he came to the bank of the bayou, where an alligator was sunning himself. The Beignet Man turned to the alligator and said:

> "Hurry, hurry as much as you can,
> I am the Beignet Man, I am!
> I've hurried away from the Mama,
> Papa, the sugarcane cutters, Peter
> Pelican, and the raccoons cleaning
> crawfish,
> And I can hurry away from you too,
> I can!"

But the crafty ole gator just kept sunning himself and turned to the Beignet Man, "I don't want to hurry anywhere, but if *you* don't hurry everyone else will catch you."

Sure enough the Beignet Man turned around and everyone was close behind. There were the raccoons, followed by Peter Pelican, then the sugarcane cutters, and finally, Papa and Mama. "Let me take you across the bayou," said the gator. The Beignet Man knew he did not have any choice so he hopped on the alligator's tail for his trip across the bayou.

As they went deeper into the bayou, the gator said, "Get on my back so you will not get wet." The Beignet Man then climbed on his back. Lo and behold, the water got deeper and the crafty ole gator said, "Get on my head so you don't get wet." The Beignet Man then climbed on his head. As they got into the middle of the bayou the gator told the Beignet Man, "Get on my snout so you don't get wet." And the Beignet Man did as he said. Just then the alligator flipped the Beignet Man up into the air and opened his big mouth. The Beignet Man disappeared in the alligator's mouth just as quick as you could blink your eyes.

That was the end of the Beignet Man!

Little Mary Plump

Little Mary Plump
Sat on a stump,
Eating her sausage and rice,
Along came a gator,
Who promised to ate her,
And frightened Mary Plump away, Yeah!

Oyster Man

Did you see the Oyster Man, the Oyster Man, the Oyster Man,
Oh, did you see the Oyster Man who lives on Shrimper's Lane?
Oh, yeah me I saw the Oyster Man, the Oyster Man, the Oyster Man,
Oh, yeah me I saw the Oyster Man who lives on Shrimper's Lane.

Petite Rouge Riding Hood

Once upon a time, there was a little girl who lived in a house on the edge of the swamp.

One day her Mama baked two sweet potato pies and placed them in a basket. She turned to the little girl, whose name was Petite Rouge Riding Hood, and said, "Your Grand Mama is feeling under the weather, so would you please deliver these pies to her? I'm quite sure she would love to have some company, but remember, do not dilly-dally along the way for I want you home before dark."

Petite Rouge Riding Hood left her house and started off for her Grand Mama's house. Her Grand Mama's house was on the other side of the swamp. Oh, how very spooky the swamp could be. She started whistling to herself and looking around when all of a sudden a bobcat stepped out into the path. "Where are you going, little girl?" asked the bobcat politely. "I'm going to deliver two sweet potato pies to my sick Grand Mama," she said. "And where does your Grand Mama live?" asked the bobcat. "In a big white house on the other side of the swamp," Petite Rouge Riding Hood answered. "Yes," said the bobcat, "I know the place well. I do hope your Grand Mama gets to feeling better soon." With that the bobcat bounced back into the trees hissing to himself. Little did Petite Rouge Riding Hood know that bobcat was taking a short cut to Grand Mama's house.

He arrived at the big white house out of breath. He knocked on the door very loudly! "Who is it?" said Grand Mama. "It's me, Petite Rouge Riding Hood," said the bobcat, trying to imitate her voice.

"Just turn the knob and come in my dear," said Grand Mama. The bobcat ran in and jumped at Grand Mama and swallowed her whole in one piece.

The bobcat then put on Grand Mama's night gown and night cap and waited for Petite Rouge Riding Hood.

Just then there was a knock on the door. "Who is it?" said the bobcat, trying to sound like Grand Mama. "It's Petite Rouge Riding Hood." "Just turn the knob and come in my dear for the door is unlocked," said the crafty old bobcat.

She came in and put the basket down. "Come here and see me, my dear," said the bobcat. "Why Grand Mama, what big eyes you have!" said Petite Rouge Riding Hood. "All the better to see you, little one," said the bobcat. "But Grand Mama, what big teeth you have!" "All the better to *eat* you with," hissed the mean old bobcat. He jumped out of bed and tried to swallow Petite Rouge Riding Hood like he had Grand Mama, but she was too quick for him. She ran outside towards the bayou.

Luckily, there was an old man shucking oysters on the dock nearby. He ran after the bobcat and tripped him. The old man noticed something moving around in the bobcat's stomach. He took his oyster knife and cut open the bobcat. Sure enough, out came Grand Mama in one piece! She was excited but all right.

The old man put Grand Mama back into her bed. He noticed the basket with the two pies lying beside the table. "What have we here?" he asked. "Some sweet potato pies that my mother baked," said Petite Rouge Riding Hood.

They all ate a piece of pie and enjoyed every bite. The old man then walked Petite Rouge Riding Hood home just before it got dark. My, oh my, Petite Rouge Riding Hood sure had a busy day and was glad to be home!

Crawfish

Crawfish! Crawfish! What is the price?
Three pounds for a dollar,
Oh, how so very nice! I garontee!

Jacques, Jacques Crawfish Eater

Jacques, Jacques Crawfish Eater,
Had a wife and couldn't keep her, no
He put her in a crawfish shell,
And there he kept her very well, yeah!

Jacques, Jacques Crawfish Eater,
Had another but didn't love her, no
Jacques learned to read and spell,
And then he loved her very well, whoo boy!

Crawfish Pie

A crawfish pie when it looks nice,
Would make one long to get a slice;
But if the taste should be so, too,
I scarce one slice would never do;
So to prevent my asking twice,
Pray, Mama, cut a great big slice.

Little Polly Sue

Little Polly Sue,
She lost her Mardi Gras shoe.
Give her another,
To match the other,
And then she can dance in two, till two.

The Fisherman's Wishes

Once upon a time, a long time ago, there was a poor fisherman and his wife who lived in a shack on the bayou.

One day while the fisherman was running his crab traps he said aloud, "I sure work hard, but it seems I never have enough money to buy the things I'd like to have." No sooner had the poor fisherman said this when out of the murky waters of the bayou appeared a beautiful mermaid. She told him in a quiet little voice, "I heard your wish and now you have three but be *very* careful how you use them." Then she disappeared under the water from where she had come.

The poor fisherman was so excited he started his motor as fast as he could and raced all the way home to his shack on the bayou. The fisherman's wife was so happy to hear the good news, for now she could have everything she had ever wanted.

As it happens, the fisherman's wife had

just finished putting supper on the table when the fisherman had come home to tell her the news, so they both decided to sit down and eat and talk about their three wishes. When the fisherman looked at his plate, he was very angry. "Turnips and greens for supper again. I wish I had a great big juicy piece of boudin sausage to eat!" Well, sure enough, a great big juicy piece of boudin appeared on his plate! His wife was really upset. "How could you be so silly and waste a wish like that? Now we have only two wishes left." The fisherman's wife just wouldn't let up; she complained and complained until finally the fisherman said, "Oh, I wish that piece of boudin sausage was stuck on you nose!" And faster than you could say jambalaya, that piece of boudin sausage was stuck to her nose.

His wife was really angry now! Not only had the fisherman wasted another wish, but she had a piece of boudin sausage stuck to her nose. They tugged and tugged and pulled and pulled, but my friend, that boudin sausage would not come off, no!

The fisherman said, "We have only one wish left. What should we wish for?" The fisherman's wife replied, "You ought to know better than that, I wish that this boudin sausage would disappear." Sure enough, in the wink of an eye, the boudin sausage was gone, but also were their three wishes. Worst of all, they didn't even get to eat that great big juicy piece of boudin sausage for supper! Pew-yah!